Lovin' Aruba!
A Kid's Guide To Oranjestad, Aruba

Photography by John D. Weigand
Poetry by Penelope Dyan

Bellissima Publishing, LLC
Jamul, California
www.bellissimapublishing.com

Copyright © 2019 by Penny D. Weigand & John D. Weigand

All rights reserved. No part of this book may be
reproduced or transmitted in any form or by any means,
electronic or mechanical, including photocopying,
recording, or by any other means, or by any information or
storage retrieval system, without permission from the publisher.

ISBN 978-1-61477-383-2
First Edition

"Both life and learning are more than a mere trip."

PENELOPE DYAN

Lovin' Aruba!
Bellissima Publishing, LLC

Introduction

Aruba is a tiny Dutch Caribbean island that sits off the coast of Venezuela; and Oranjestad, a Dutch name, translated, means "Orange Town" . . . although it should be noted that our author and photographer didn't actually see any oranges growing on orange trees there. Oranjestad is the capital and largest city on the small Island of Aruba, and is actually named after King William I of the Netherlands, the crown Prince of Orange-Nassau. So the name of the city probably, and more than likely, has nothing to do with either oranges or orange trees, and is a subject into which a discerning, learning kid may be curious, and into which subject he or she may want to delve.

However, this book isn't about that, because this fun,. 'learn to read' book, filled with word recognition, word repetition and rhyme, is meant to increase reading skills and vocabulary and show this place the way a kid will see it. Its extra-large print and carry along size (perfect for a kid-sized backpack) makes this book a perfect travel carry-on. Written by award winning author, attorney and former teacher, Penelope Dyan, with photography by John D. Weigand, this is a book with a purpose; and there is a free, fun music video that goes along with this book on Bellissimavideo's YouTube channel!

Lovin' Aruba!
Bellissima Publishing, LLC

Lovin' Aruba!
A Kid's Guide To Oranjestad, Aruba

Photography by John D. Weigand
Poetry by Penelope Dyan

When you arrive in Oranjestad, Aruba
you will get a kid's eye view
of the blue of the Caribbean Sea,
and of what lies ahead of you!

As you get closer you see even more, and Mom announces, "I can't wait to go shopping at an Oranjestad, Aruba store!"

Yes . . Mom says she just can't wait,
and she ALREADY feels like
it might be TOO late!
Dad laughs; and he says,
"Well, I guess it's true . . .
that there is NEVER quite enough
shopping for YOU!"

Mom looks out over the bridge
of the cruise ship
as it PREPARES to dock.
And THEN she checks the hands
on the lower deck ship clock.
Sis says, with just a little despair,
"I hope MOM doesn't buy ME
MORE clean underwear!"
AND . . . then (for good measure)
Sis REMINDS Mom
that she washed ALL of her underwear
in the cabin room SINK,
just to make sure
that it DIDN'T stink!

You see a truck that says
"I love Aruba!"
AND then you all hop right aboard
an orange and blue trolley!
As the bell rings out at each stop,
you feel happy AND quite jolly!

You HOP out of the trolley.
AND Mom hands her purse
to a shiny, black COW!
Mom isn't worried the cow will
open the purse,
because the cow
simply doesn't know HOW!

Then you see something else,
of course,
right ahead of you stands
a bright BLUE HORSE!

You keep walking down the street!
AND then you stop
and you have something to eat!

And then, finally AND after all,
Mom finds a VERY lovely shopping mall!

And right there, outside on the street,
there is even MORE!
Mom buys herself a dress . . .
AND a pair of maracas
at an outdoor, sidewalk STORE!

And you can ONLY smile
when you see a man resting,
AND probably asleep,
just sitting right there
next to HIS shop on the STREET!

And as the sun sets in the west
(as the 'old-time' cowboys say)
Dad says,
"It's NOW high time
that WE get 'a moving' on OUR way."
And Sis happily plays the maracas
Mom bought,
without a single care,
just happy mom DIDN'T buy HER
MORE underwear!

"Look around! There is always something to see, even in the clouds."

PENELOPE DYAN

www.ingramcontent.com/pod-product-compliance
Ingram Content Group UK Ltd.
Pitfield, Milton Keynes, MK11 3LW, UK
UKHW060134240426
12048UKWH00002B/27